Lincoln's Birthday

Dennis Brindell Fradin

—Best Holiday Books—

ENSLOW PUBLISHERS, INC.
Bloy St. & Ramsey Ave.   P.O. Box 38
Box 777   Aldershot
Hillside, N.J. 07205   Hants GU12 6BP
U.S.A.   U.K.

For my dear son, Anthony Derrick Fradin

Copyright © 1990 by Enslow Publishers, Inc.

Library of Congress Cataloging-in-Publication Data

Fradin, Dennis B.
    Lincoln's Birthday / by Dennis Brindell Fradin.
    p. cm. — (Best holiday books)
    Includes index.
    Summary: Discusses how the achievements of our nation's sixteenth president
led to the present-day celebration of his birth.
    ISBN 0-89490-250-4
    1. Lincoln Day—Juvenile literature. 2. Lincoln, Abraham,1809-1865—Juvenile
literature. [1. Lincoln Day. 2. Lincoln, Abraham, 1809-1865.] I. Title. II. Series:
Fradin, Dennis B. Best holiday books.
E457.7.F82 1990
973.7'092—dc20
[B]   89-7665
                                                                                          CIP
                                                                                           AC

Printed in the United States of America

10 9 8 7 6 5 4 3 2 1

Illustration Credits:
Cameramann International, Ltd.: p. 40; Tom Dunnington: p. 15; Photo by Jerry
Hennen: p. 17; Historical Pictures Service, Chicago: p. 13; Illinois Secretary of
State's Office: p. 4; Courtesy of the Illinois State Historical Library: pp. 7, 19, 25;
Bequest of Henry C. Lewis, The University of Michigan Museum of Art: p. 9; Library
of Congress: pp. 12, 21, 23, 27, 29, 30, 32, 34, 36.

Cover Illustration by Charlott Nathan

Contents

This Lincoln portrait was lost in a locked, painted-over room in the Illinois State Capitol for many years.

A Great President

The leader of the United States is called the president. The president commands the U.S. armed forces and meets with world leaders. Good presidents have helped the nation win wars and survive hard times. The sixteenth president, Abraham Lincoln, was one of the greatest people the nation has ever produced.

President Lincoln kept the United States from splitting apart during the Civil War. He also took steps to end slavery. Because Lincoln did so much, his birthday is a holiday in many states. Some states hold the holiday right on his birthday—February 12. Others celebrate Lincoln's Birthday on a nearby date in February. Each February, millions of schoolchildren learn about what Lincoln did to earn this honor.

Abraham Lincoln's Early Years

Abraham Lincoln was born on February 12, 1809, in a log cabin about 50 miles south of Louisville, Kentucky. His parents were Nancy and Thomas Lincoln. He also had a sister, Sarah, who was two years older than he.

When Abraham was two, he and his family moved a few miles away to Knob Creek. Abraham was helping with the farm work by the time he was six or seven. From time to time he and Sarah went to school, where they learned a little reading, writing, and math.

On December 11, 1816, Indiana entered the Union as the nineteenth state. Thomas Lincoln was having trouble over ownership of his Kentucky lands. He also hated slavery. At the time,

Kentucky was one of the states that allowed slavery. Indiana was one of those that did not. The Lincolns moved to Indiana near the time that it became a state. They settled at Little Pigeon Creek in southern Indiana.

Now almost eight, Abraham was strong enough to swing an ax. He and his father

This cabin near Hodgenville, Kentucky, is thought to look like and contain logs from Abraham Lincoln's birthplace.

chopped down trees, then used the logs to build a new cabin. Abraham also helped Thomas Lincoln clear fields and plant crops.

The family had lived in Indiana for about two years when Mrs. Lincoln came down with "milk sickness." It came from drinking milk from cows that had eaten poisonous plants. Nancy Lincoln called Abraham and Sarah to her bedside. She told them to be kind and good people. Soon after that, she died.

Nine-year-old Abraham grieved for his mother. He was also upset that a preacher hadn't given her a funeral. Weeks later a preacher came by and said a service over Nancy Lincoln's grave. That helped Abraham feel more at peace about her death.

Meanwhile, 11-year-old Sarah had become the woman of the house. She cooked, cleaned, and made clothes. But Thomas felt that his children needed a stepmother. A year after his wife's death, Thomas went to Kentucky. There he visited a woman he knew, Sarah Bush Johnston. Sally, as she was called, was a widow

THE BOY LINCOLN
BY
EASTMAN JOHNSON
1824 - 1906

Abraham loved books and has often been portrayed reading. This painting dates back to 1868.

with three children. Sally and Thomas Lincoln married, then went to Indiana with her children.

Abraham liked his new family. In fact, he and his stepmother grew to love each other deeply. Abraham had not gone to school for some time. Seeing how bright he was, Sally Lincoln sent him to school. There were few teachers in the wilderness, though. In all, Abraham spent only about a year in backwoods schools.

Abraham learned without going to school. He loved books and read whenever he could. He read before and after his farm work. He sat under a tree and read during his lunch break. There were few books in backwoods Indiana. If Abraham heard that a neighbor had a new book, he would walk miles to borrow it.

Abraham also liked to tell "tall tales," or made-up stories, to his friends. A book he found on public speaking was a big help. He became so good at telling stories that many people would gather to hear him.

Abraham Goes Out
Into the World

When he was 16, Abraham was over six feet tall.⁺ inches
He was very thin and very strong. He earned 25
cents a day building rail fences and working on
neighbors' farms. He gave the money to his father.

In 1828, Abraham received a terrible blow
when his sister, Sarah, died. That same year a
neighbor hired his own son and Abraham to take
some goods more than 1,000 miles to New
Orleans, Louisiana.

The two young men built a flatboat, then
loaded their cargo onto it. Down the Ohio River
they went, and then down the Mississippi River.
They almost did not reach New Orleans. Near
the city they were attacked by a gang, but they
managed to fight them off.

Abraham Lincoln chopping up logs. Can you tell what he plans to do when he takes a break from his work?

New Orleans was the first big city Abraham had seen. He liked its crowded streets and busy port. But New Orleans' slave market troubled him. He wondered how Southerners could allow so evil a thing as slavery to exist.

After selling their cargo, the young men took a steamboat home. Abraham gave the 24 dollars

Abraham was very upset when he saw New Orleans' slave market.

he had earned from the three-month trip to his father.

The Lincolns had not done well in Indiana. In 1830 they headed to Illinois, settling on the Sangamon River near Decatur. Abraham helped his father build a new log cabin and farm.

Soon Abraham felt ready to start his own life. In early 1831 he made another flatboat trip to New Orleans. The man who hired Abraham to make this journey liked him a lot. He gave Abraham a job in a store he owned in New Salem, Illinois, not far from Springfield.

Twenty-two-year-old Abraham Lincoln moved to New Salem. He worked behind the store counter in the daytime. At night he slept at the back of the store. Abraham became popular in New Salem. Many of its 100 people visited the store to hear his stories. And Abraham ran races and entered other sporting events in the town.

One day a young man named Jack Armstrong challenged Abraham to wrestle him. Armstrong was New Salem's wrestling champ and the

The fight between Abraham Lincoln and Jack Armstrong

leader of a local gang. On the day of the match, a crowd gathered. The two men fought for a while, and then suddenly Armstrong smashed his boot down on Lincoln's foot. Enraged, Abraham lifted Armstrong into the air and threw him down. Armstrong's gang then came toward Lincoln, ready to fight. But Armstrong stood up and shook Abraham's hand. After that, the two of them were friends.

Abraham liked thinking better than fighting, though. He joined the New Salem Debating Society. Its members argued over politics and other matters. Mentor Graham, a New Salem schoolmaster, belonged to this club. Mr. Graham thought that Abraham was bright but uneducated. He gave him books to read. Business was so poor at the store that Abraham had plenty of time to read them.

The store went out of business in 1832. That year Abraham ran for office for the first time. He hoped to be elected as an Illinois state lawmaker. But in the summer of 1832 he lost the election.

Lincoln's New Salem State Park in Illinois has a replica of the town where Abraham Lincoln lived as a young man.

"Honest Abe,"
Politician and Lawyer

Twenty-three-year-old Abraham Lincoln did not know what to do with his life. He wanted to be a lawyer, but he felt he did not have the schooling to study law. He decided to try storekeeping again.

Abraham bought a store with a partner. It soon failed and his partner died, leaving Abraham with unpaid bills. Many people would have tried to avoid paying the debt. But Abraham promised to pay back all the money. Eventually he did pay it back. Later he was called "Honest Abe" because he always kept his word.

After the store closed, Lincoln worked at

many jobs. He became New Salem's postmaster. He chopped down trees and made fence rails. He also studied books that helped him become a surveyor—someone who figures land boundaries. Lincoln laid out some towns and roads that still exist in Illinois. All his jobs helped Abraham earn a living and pay his debt.

Inside of the New Salem store that Abraham Lincoln owned with a partner

In 1834 Abraham ran for the Illinois legislature again. This time he was elected. He went to Vandalia, which was then the Illinois capital. Lincoln served eight years as an Illinois lawmaker. He helped get the Illinois capital moved to Springfield. He worked to build canals and railroads in Illinois. And he opposed slavery, but not as strongly as he would later.

Meanwhile, Abraham studied to become a lawyer. He did this on his own, as he had done with surveying. He became a lawyer in 1836. His office was in Springfield, but he also went to courthouses across the countryside. He gained fame in Illinois for arguing his cases well.

Soon after moving to Springfield, Abraham had met young Mary Todd. The two of them were married in late 1842. They lived in a big house in Springfield where they raised four sons: Robert, Eddie, Willie, and Tad.

In 1846, Abraham ran for the U.S. House of Representatives and won. Nothing was easy for him, though. Partly because he had opposed the

Mary Todd Lincoln

Mexican War, many Illinois people turned against him. He did not run for re-election in 1848.

Abraham Lincoln returned to Springfield in 1849. He thought he would never seek office again. But in the 1850s the slavery issue made him go back to politics. White Southerners used black slaves to grow crops. Most white Southerners wanted to keep slavery. They also wanted new states to decide for themselves if they wanted slavery. Many Northerners—and some Southerners—hated slavery. They hoped to end slavery, or at least outlaw it in new states.

Lincoln returned to politics as an enemy of slavery. In 1856 he joined the new Republican Party, which opposed slavery. The Republicans picked him to run for U.S. senator from Illinois two years later.

Lincoln's foe, Stephen A. Douglas, was far more accepting of slavery than he was. The two men traveled around the state of Illinois arguing about slavery. These talks were called the

The earliest known photograph of Lincoln, made in 1846 when he was 37 years old

Lincoln-Douglas Debates. They were held between August and October of 1858.

Calling slavery "evil," Lincoln did very well at these debates. Newspapers reported his words, and his fame spread from Illinois to the rest of the nation. He became known as "Long Abe" or the "Tall Sucker" because he was almost six feet, four inches tall.

Abraham lost a close election to Douglas in November of 1858. "I am too big to cry," he said about this loss, "and too badly hurt to laugh." However, he vowed to go on fighting slavery.

Lincoln was asked to speak around the country after this defeat. In February of 1860 he made a great speech in New York City. He ended with the words: "Let us have faith that right makes might, and in that faith let us, to the end, dare to do our duty as we understand it." He was saying that doing the right thing (on slavery and other issues) would make people strong. And he hoped people would have the courage to do what was right.

One of the Lincoln-Douglas debates of 1858. This one was at Charleston, Illinois.

The Sixteenth President

The election for U.S. president was coming up in November of 1860. The Republicans held a convention that May. They chose Abraham Lincoln as their candidate.

Before the election, 11-year-old Grace Bedell wrote Lincoln a letter from New York State. Grace said a beard would make him look better. Lincoln took her advice. The beard became a Lincoln trademark. He is shown with a beard on U.S. five-dollar bills and pennies.

Abraham Lincoln had often failed in his life. But he easily won the 1860 election. He and Mary Lincoln moved with their sons Willie and Tad to the White House in Washington, D.C. Robert was at college. Eddie had died a few years earlier at the age of four.

Lincoln grew a beard on the advice of 11-year-old Grace Bedell.

President and Mrs. Lincoln gave Willie and Tad a lot of freedom. The boys rode their pony on the White House grounds. Tad was allowed to keep a pet goat. Tragically, Willie died in early 1862. After that, the president hardly let Tad out of his sight. He and Tad took walks together through Washington, D.C. The president bought Tad toys and gingerbread on their walks. President Lincoln even let Tad play in his office during important meetings.

Lincoln faced huge problems from the start of his first term. White Southerners feared that Lincoln would take steps against slavery. Soon after his election, Southern states had begun to leave the United States. They proclaimed their own country, the Confederate States of America (or Confederacy).

The president and most Northerners felt that the South had no right to leave the United States. But the South was ready to fight to establish the Confederacy. The Civil War began on April 12, 1861. On one side were the Confederate (or Southern) states. Against them

From left Abraham, Mary Todd, Tad, and Robert Lincoln. Again
Abraham is with his trademark, a book.

Many Civil War soldiers were little more than boys. This young Confederate soldier was killed in 1862.

were the Union (or Northern) states, led by President Lincoln.

Abraham Lincoln was a man of peace. Years *but he hated slavery.* before, people had turned against him for opposing the Mexican War. But now he was leading the Union in the bloodiest war in U.S. history. Both sides together lost about half a million men in the Civil War. That is about the number of Americans who died in all other wars combined.

The Union had more men and supplies. But the South had better generals, and most of the battles were fought on the South's home ground. For several years it looked as though the South might win.

On January 1, 1863, in the middle of the war, Lincoln issued the Emancipation Proclamation. This paper freed the Confederacy's slaves. And it paved the way for ending slavery in the whole United States several years later. Also in 1863, there was a turning point in the war. It was the Battle of Gettysburg, fought in Pennsylvania on July 1–3, 1863.

The Battle of Gettysburg was one of the bloodiest battles of the Civil War.

Union forces won the Battle of Gettysburg. A few months later, a cemetery was dedicated for the soldiers buried there. Lincoln gave his famous Gettysburg Address at this ceremony. In this speech he said that the war was being waged so that "government of the people, by the people, for the people, shall not perish from the earth."

The Union finally won the war on April 9, 1865. President Lincoln had kept the nation from splitting apart. By the end of the war he had been president for over four years, having been re-elected in 1864. But he had been so troubled by the war that he looked 20 years older after those four years.

President Lincoln was a loving father. Here he is with his son Tad.

Lincoln's Death

Less than a week of life remained to Abraham Lincoln after the war ended. During his last days he planned to rebuild the South and end the hatred between North and South.

On Friday, April 14, 1865, Lincoln told his wife that he had never felt so happy in his life. That night the two of them went to a play at Ford's Theatre in Washington, D.C. Shortly after ten o'clock, a man with a gun came up to where the president was sitting. The man, John Wilkes Booth, blamed Lincoln for the South's defeat. Booth fired his gun at Lincoln's head. The president slumped over, very badly wounded. Booth ran away but was later killed.

The president was carried to a building across the street. Doctors treated him all night, with no success. Abraham Lincoln died at 7:22 on the morning of April 15, 1865. When Lincoln stopped breathing, Secretary of War Edwin Stanton said: "Now he belongs to the ages." When Tad learned about what had happened he cried, "They killed my pa! They killed my pa!"

John Wilkes Booth murdering President Lincoln

Lincoln's Birthday Becomes a Holiday

The year after Lincoln's death, 1866, a big ceremony was held in Washington, D.C., to honor his memory. It took place on February 12, Lincoln's birthday. Andrew Johnson, who had become president upon Lincoln's death, attended. So did many lawmakers and citizens. Speeches about Lincoln were the highlight of the ceremony. This was the first step in making Lincoln's birthday a holiday.

Because Lincoln spent most of his life there, Illinois calls itself the Land of Lincoln. In 1892, Illinois became the first state to make Lincoln's birthday a holiday. Since then, many other states have done the same.

Today, over 30 states celebrate Lincoln's

Birthday. Some of them celebrate it on February 12. By chance, President George Washington was also born in February. Some states honor both Washington and Lincoln on the third Monday in February. They call the holiday Presidents' Day.

Schoolchildren and Lincoln's Birthday

Each year, children in thousands of schools learn about Abraham Lincoln near the time of his birthday. Their teachers read them books and tell them about Lincoln's life. Then the children write stories and poems about Lincoln. In some schools, the children make costumes and act out scenes from Lincoln's life.

Drawing or painting pictures of the sixteenth president is another popular school activity. Fortunately we know what Lincoln looked like, because he was the first president to be photographed often. Most children draw him wearing the beard that 11-year-old Grace Bedell asked him to grow. Making a model of the log cabin

This boy has made a model of the log cabin where Abraham Lincoln was born.

where Lincoln was born is another popular art project.

In their music classes, children may learn songs about Lincoln and the Civil War. One of them is called "The Battle Hymn of the Republic." It was written by Julia Ward Howe in 1861, soon after the Civil War began.

Since 1976, February has been Black History Month in the United States. Many school-children learn about famous black people during the month. And around February 12, they learn what Abraham Lincoln and the Civil War meant to black history.

The Big Day Arrives

Some schools and some businesses close on Lincoln's Birthday. Special ceremonies are held in numerous cities and towns. People read Lincoln's famous speeches aloud to crowds. Bands play. And some people make their own speeches about the sixteenth president.

In Springfield, Illinois, where Lincoln is buried, there is a wreath-laying ceremony at his tomb. At the Lincoln Memorial in Washington, D.C., a band plays and the Gettysburg Address is read aloud.

Throughout the country, there are a number of Abraham Lincoln clubs. Their members enjoy studying and talking about Lincoln. On his birthday, many of these clubs do something special, such as bringing in an author to speak about Lincoln.

Many TV stations run special shows about Lincoln on his birthday. These include programs about Lincoln's life and old movies about him. Two of the best-known old movies about the sixteenth president are *Young Mr. Lincoln* with Henry Fonda and *Abe Lincoln in Illinois* with Raymond Massey.

Lincoln's Birthday is also a time when many families discuss what the sixteenth president meant to the nation. Today the North and South are both part of the United States. And there has been no slavery in the United States for over 100 years. Isn't February 12 a good day to remember the great president who helped provide us with these blessings?

Glossary

candidate—a person who runs for office

capital—the place where laws are made for a nation or state

Civil War—the war the Northern states fought against the Southern states from 1861 to 1865

Confederate States of America—the name for the Southern states during the Civil War

convention—a big meeting

debate—an organized argument with rules

election—an event in which people vote

Emancipation Proclamation—a paper President Lincoln issued that paved the way for ending slavery in the United States

grieve—to feel very sad

legislature—a body of lawmakers

million—a thousand thousand (1,000,000)

perish—to die or disappear

poisonous—something that is very harmful

president—an important leader; the United States' main leader is called the president

slavery—the practice of owning people

surveyor—someone who figures land boundaries

Union—the name for the Northern states during the Civil War

White House—the home of the president of the United States

widow—a woman whose husband is dead

wounded—this usually means hurt by someone else

wreath—a round decoration usually made of plants

Index